Otto von Frisch

Canaries

Everything about Purchase, Care,
Diseases, Nutrition, and Song

With 25 Color Photographs by Outstanding Animal
Photographers and 35 Drawings by Fritz W. Köhler

Translated by Helgard Niewisch, D.V.M.

Barron's
New York/London/Toronto/Sydney

First English language edition published in 1983 by
Barron's Educational Series, Inc.
© 1979 by Gräfe and Unzer GmbH, Munich,
West Germany

The title of the German book is *Kanarienvögel*.

All inquiries should be addressed to:
Barron's Educational Series, Inc.
250 Wireless Boulevard
Hauppauge, New York 11788

International Standard Book No. 0-8120-2614-4

Library of Congress Cataloging in Publication Data

Frisch, Otto von.
    Canaries.

    Translation of: Kanarienvögel.
    Bibliography: p.
    Includes index.
    Summary: A guide to caring for a pet canary,
from things to consider before buying to understanding your pet's psychology.
    1. Canaries. [1. Canaries] I. Köhler, Fritz W.,
ill. I. Title.
SF463.F7513 1983   636.6′862   83-2777
ISBN 0-8120-2614-4

PRINTED IN HONG KONG
89   490   98

Professor Otto von Frisch
Son of the Nobel Prize winner Dr. Karl von Frisch,
Professor Otto von Frisch grew up surrounded by
animals of all kinds. A tame jackdaw named Tobby
and other birds were among his boyhood
companions.
    Otto von Frisch studied biology in Munich and,
for one year, in the United States. He wrote his
doctoral dissertation in 1956 on "Brood Biology
and Early Development in Curlews." Dr. von Frisch
is director of the Museum of Natural History in
Braunschweig and professor of zoology at the
Braunschweig Technical University. In 1973 Dr. von
Frisch received the German Juvenile Book Award
for his work *1,000 Tricks of Camouflage*.

Cover design: Constanze Reithmayr-Frank

Front cover: (left) Bright yellow canary
              (center) Copper red (mat) canary
              (right) Pale yellow canary
Inside front cover: A pair of bright orange reds
Inside back cover: Two Harz Rollers: (left) pale
              yellow; (right) pale red
Back cover: (above) Color canaries, bright orange
              and bright yellow
              (below, from left to right) Border,
              Norwich, Northern Dutch, and
              German Crested canaries

Photographs
Bielfeld: pages 9, 55
Coleman/Burton: Inside front cover, page 56
(below)
Coleman/Lambrechts: page 56 (above)
Dr. Jesse: page 38, back cover (above right)
Reinhard: Front cover; pages 10, 27, 28, 37; inside
back cover, back cover (above left, below)

Contents

Preface

Apart from parakeets, canaries are the most commonly owned pets. They are favorites not only because of their beauty but also because of their lovely songs. No other cage bird has a voice equal to that of the songster from the Canary Islands, which is generally sold today as a Roller canary. The first thing a bird lover about to buy a young canary will therefore want to know is whether his bird will sing.

Which canary breeds should you buy if you want to have a bird that sings well? That is the first of many questions this small book will help you answer.

Professor Otto von Frisch, son of the Nobel Prize winner Dr. Karl von Frisch, knows all about keeping canaries from his own experience. He begins by explaining to the reader what a canary is, and he shows, from a "bird's eye perspective," how the canary perceives his new unfeathered companion and partner. As an experienced ornithologist Dr. von Frisch will help the canary owner and the rest of the family deal with the daily business — and problems — of keeping a pet canary. Citing many practical examples, he will teach the new owner how to care for and feed the canary properly, what to do in case of disease, how to deal with molting, and what precautions to take to prevent accidents and injuries when the bird flies loose in your home.

A canary will develop into a good singer only if he feels at home in his surroundings — if his owner creates conditions suitable for birds. An understanding of bird nature and behavior are essential for the proper handling of canaries, and in the special chapter "Understanding Canaries" these topics are discussed in detail.

The chapters "Canary Pairing and Breeding" and "Canary Breeds" are written especially for experienced canary owners. They contain rules for breeding canaries successfully. Breeding birds is not a simple matter and a thorough understanding of the principles involved is essential for this hobby.

The Songster from the Canary Islands

History of the Canary

When the Spanish discovered and conquered the Canary Islands toward the end of the fifteenth century, they must have taken pleasure in the varied melodious songs of the native birds there. In any case, these conquerors were the first to introduce canaries to Europe, where they were soon bred domestically. Spanish monks became expert breeders. They soon developed a brisk business dealing in these small, yellow-green songbirds. They sold only male birds abroad, and consequently their clientele in France, Italy, and England remained dependent on them. This is why the price for canaries was very high and only wealthy people could afford them. Ladies were especially fond of canaries and liked to keep them in expensive cages. By the seventeenth century, however, the Italians and the English had succeeded in breaking the Spanish monopoly on female canaries. Just how they succeeded in obtaining the females was never disclosed and remains a mystery today. Breeders soon created the first color mutations, and the yellow checkered strain was established. The breeding of canaries spread to other countries and flourished especially in Tyrolia, Switzerland, Holland, and Germany.

Development of Canary Breeding

Quality and beauty of song were not the only goals breeders pursued; in many areas emphasis was placed early on obtaining specific colorations and other physical characteristics. For a time the so-called "frilled" canary, a bird sporting curly feathers, was the rage. But in most highly specialized breeds of this kind, the quality of song that has been previously achieved by painstaking effort suffers or is lost.

Fancy breeds popular in the rococo period, e.g., canaries with hooded heads, feather ruffs, elongated bodies, or unnatural wing postures, are practically unknown today. Modern breeders concentrate primarily on coloration and singing ability and aim to combine these two characteristics in the same strain. The pure yellow canary has been in existence since the sixteenth century, while the red canary dates back only to the beginning of this century.

The Harz Roller and Similar Breeds

This type of canary is found most often in pet stores and homes. Systematic breeding of the strain was started in the nineteenth century in

The Songster from the Canary Islands

Europe, and at the turn of the century these birds were sold by the millions all over the world.

The names St. Andreasberg Roller and Harz Roller denote the original breeding sites in Germany. Canaries were first introduced into the Harz Mountain region by Tyrolean miners who used them to detect dangerous gases in the mines. The German place names are often added to the denotation of show birds to emphasize high quality background. Other labels such as Opera Singer, etc., are used to draw attention to the birds' high singing quality; they are neither standard nor uniform. The American Singer is now a world famous Roller.

Another favorite and readily available canary breed in the United States is the Chopper. Its song is louder and more natural though less sensitive than the Roller's, but it is still very beautiful. And this type of bird usually costs a lot less. Beautiful colors are also being developed in these breeds.

Canary Breeds

Since modern canaries have been domesticated for over five hundred years, it is natural that their original color, song, and behavior have undergone changes. Many different strains have been developed, and breeders everywhere have tried to come up with pure breeds; some emphasize song, others shape or color. Today there are three distinct categories of canary breeds:

Song canaries
Color canaries
Type canaries

A fourth category is that of the *hybrid canaries,* crosses between canaries and wild finch strains.

There are approximately forty major pure breeds, not counting crosses with wild birds. Most of these breeds are rarely encountered in ordinary bird or pet stores. Here you will find the "yellow" and the "red" the most common representatives of the color canaries and, of course, good singers like the Harz Roller.

Before I introduce the various breeds, I should like to warn the amateur that professional breeders are less than happy when their painstakingly developed pure strains are mixed and the results end up in pet stores. If you seriously consider breeding canaries, you should decide which breed or breeds you are interested in and watch out for purity of strain. If all you want is to raise one group of nestlings to watch their development, you need not worry about the background of your canaries. The colorful offspring of a red male and a yellow female, or vice versa, may even give you the side benefit of an interesting lesson in genetics.

For the serious student of canary breeding there are voluminous treatises on the different canary strains where each tone of the characteristic songs and the color of each feather are described in detail. For the beginner or the owner of a single bird, such a wealth of information is overwhelming. In this book I will therefore describe characteristics of breeds only to the extent useful for choosing and buying a pet canary.

Song Canaries

Undoubtedly the *Harz Roller* is the most common and most popular song canary. His song is not as loud and shrill as that of his less aristocratic cousins; it is also considerably more varied than that of other song canaries (see page 8).

A more recent breed is the *Belgian Waterslager.* This canary is somewhat larger and has an even more varied song vocabulary, but not all tones are as melodious as those of the Harz

Plate 1   *Above: A Harz Roller and a bright copper* ▷
red canary.   Center: Gloster Fancy Corona and two
Northern Dutch canaries.   Below: A Munich
posture canary and a silver Lizard.

Roller. The *American Singer* is not only one of the most outstanding song canaries, but it also displays beautiful color and posture. The recent color and song breeds also aim for a combination of these qualities. These lovely birds with beautiful voices are ideal for bird lovers who want a single canary.

Let me emphasize again that any male canary of whatever background may sing well and pleasantly. If song is important to you, be sure to listen long enough to a bird before you decide to buy it.

Song Structure and the Training of Singing Birds

I will introduce here only the famous song of the Harz Roller. This canary was bred solely for purity of song, and all the imperfect, rasping, or shrill notes of ordinary canaries have been eliminated by breeding.

The song consists of four main verses or "tours": The *hollow roll* is what gave the Harz Roller its name. In this tour, "ue," "o," or "oo" sounds are sung in combination with a rolling "r." The lower the pitch, the better. In the *bass roll,* the deepest tour of the complete song, only the "o" is rolled. The *flute* consists of a soft "due-due-due" or "doo-doo-doo" that is repeated three to five times. The *hollow bell* resembles the roll, but the "r" is re-

placed by the softer "l," and the individual sounds can be perceived as separate units. This tour sounds something like 'lue-lue-lue" or "lo-lo-lo" and includes both upward and downward shifts in pitch. The Harz Roller's repertoire also includes a number of other notes and tours, and together with the basic tours, they constitute the typical song of this breed. The best Rollers sing with their beaks almost completely closed.

Figure 1   *The song of the Harz Roller consists of four verses or "tours." One of these, the "hollow roll," gave this breed its name.*

Selecting stock for ability to sing and raising young songbirds demand hard work and a good ear. Soon after the young male birds become independent and are housed in separate large cages or aviaries they will try out their songs and start to compete with each other. These first attempts are quite clumsy, but they are a sure sign for sexing young birds.

After the first (postjuvenal) molt most young cocks are placed in individual "song cages" in which each bird can "study" and improve his song. During this period, the birds cannot see each other, but they can hear each other, which stimulates their desire to excel. A breeder will often place a good and experienced singer among the "students" for them to imitate, but this is not absolutely necessary. The songs develop perfectly well even in the absence of a model.

The method of using a canary "teacher" was employed successfully by the Tyrolean miners who were the first to raise purebred Roller canaries. The Tyroleans also used another trick: The most promising canary "students" were brought together with a nightingale "teacher" whose famous trills they would learn to imitate.

In pet stores, good singers are normally kept in individual cages. This gives the potential buyer a good chance to listen to the birds he is interested in. I will explain later (see page 19) why it is not advisable to keep a canary in a small song cage after purchase.

Color Canaries

The ancestor of all our domestic canaries is the wild canary. Its coloring is green and yellow with black streaking and brownish black wings. The color canaries of today evolved from mutations (sudden genetic changes) in the original coloring. Some of these mutations were then picked and propagated through careful selection and crossing of stock. Obviously, not all canaries are yellow. And among yellow canaries there are different types. They are divided into light, medium, and dark yellow. Then there are white, red, orange red, brown, silver brown, and orange brown canaries, as well as other shades. Still, the average person and the novice bird owner tend to think of canaries as yellow. Maybe this is because the first mutations of wild canaries were yellow, and yellow canaries are still bred and distributed in the largest numbers. Also, yellow canaries are usually the least expensive.

But pet stores usually also carry whitish and red or reddish canaries. What color canary you choose is a matter of taste. The details of breeding for a certain color involve a highly complex science. Some color characteristics are dominant. That means — in simplified terms — that the color is passed on in the genes and actually appears in the offspring. Other characteristics are recessive, which means that they are part of the genetic heritage but are not outwardly

Canary Breeds

manifest. The difference between dominant and recessive traits plays an important role in the crossing and breeding of strains, and a thorough knowledge of the principles and details involved is essential if one wants to maintain the purity of a line or breed a new strain. Sometimes, of course, chance enters the game in the form of an unexpected mutation.

Type Canaries (Posture Canaries)

Lizard Canaries are a class of bird somewhere between color canaries and type or posture canaries. Their body structure is not particularly unusual, however. The characteristic feature of this breed is the dark, scale-shaped pattern of the plumage, which resembles the markings of a lizard, hence the name. These birds were probably bred as early as the sixteenth century in England.

Typical posture canaries like the Crested Canary and the Gloster Fancy Corona have more or less pronounced crests or "wigs." The German Hooded Canaries belong to this same group. Some people like these breeds with their unusual and rather unnatural feather formations and find them cute, but it is difficult to see the beauty of other, even more artificial looking strains like the *Bossu Belge,* the *Scotch Fancy,* the *Southern*

Dutch, or the *Milan Frill.* These birds are bred to exhibit upright posture, slim shape, and/or whirls of long feathers on certain parts of the body. Not much of the original appearance is left, and a bird with such out-rageous plumage would find it hard to survive in the wild. Its feathers would get drenched in the rain, and it would probably freeze to death in cold weather. In addition it would be a poor flyer.

Hybrids

So far we have talked about breeds and crosses of different strains, i.e., birds that may look quite different from each other but that belong to the same species. If, however, a canary is bred with a wild bird of the finch family, this is a crossing of different species. In nature members of different species hardly ever mate. Their way of life and behavior differ too much, even if they are closely related. Also, there are usually enough potential sexual partners of the same species available.

Among domesticated birds the pairing of different species is not un-common. After all, their living conditions leave the birds little choice. If you keep a canary in the same cage with a finch and neither has a partner of his own species, the two will mate

Canary Breeds

Figure 2 *Left: a piebald canary; right: a Dutch "type" canary.*

and raise young. These are hybrids and are usually unable to reproduce. However, male offspring of canaries and members of closely related finch families, such as the serins *(Serinus serinus),* are fertile. The cross between canaries and the colorful European Goldfinches *(Carduelis carduelis)* is also popular. Other birds that can be mated with canaries are the European Green Finch *(Carduelis chloris),* the Redpoll *(Acanthis flammea),* the European Purple Finch *(Carpodactus erythrinus),* as well as various American finches. But getting a pair of birds of divergent backgrounds used to each other requires a lot more time and patience than mating a pair of canaries. Wild birds are shier and adjust less easily to living in an aviary, let alone in a small cage. They are also fussier about food and nesting materials. Often the wild males are more passionate and aggressive than male canaries and are rougher on the females. But a wild male and a domesticated female is a combination preferable to the reverse one. Wild females are so particular about nesting materials that they often refuse to build a nest.

There is a wide variety of wild canary breeds. In Africa alone, twenty-seven strains and many more sub-strains are known. There is a flourishing trade in these birds, and today they are found everywhere.

Considerations Before You Buy

Basic Considerations

First of all, consider realistically whether you — or whoever the canary is intended for — are really able to take care of a pet, even if it is "only" a bird. Housing the canary will be no great problem. A cage appropriate for a canary (see page 19) can be placed in just about any home or room, as long as a few basic conditions are met. But even a canary needs looking after. You have to feed him, water him, clean his cage, pay some attention to him — all this every day. In this he is like any other pet — cat, dog, or bird. The fact that the canary is so popular does not mean that he requires no care, that you can forget about him, leaving him sitting in the dark for three days or letting him go without food.

Remember, too, that a canary, small as he may be, will share your home and will be hard to get away from, particularly if you live in a one-room apartment. He may get on your nerves, or vice versa. Even the tap tap of his hopping from perch to perch may drive you crazy if you are tense to start with, and people have been known to tire occasionally of the canary's song. The bird, for his part, will be less than happy if you are a chain smoker.

I am not saying that any of this will happen, but it might. I have some experience with keeping birds, and I would like to prevent you from finding yourself in the situation of wishing you had never brought your pet home. An animal is not an object that can simply be gotten rid of or put aside for a while. Any animal, including a canary, is most at ease and comfortable in the place it is used to. You can't just open the window and set your canary "free" when you want to go on vacation. At best it would live until fall; more likely, a cat or another predator will spot it long before that thanks to its bright coloring, or it will fall victim to some other disaster.

Speaking of vacations, it is important to consider before you buy a canary who will look after him when you are away from home either on vacation or for other reasons (see page 40). Ordinarily you will want to leave your canary at home rather than take him along on a trip (see page 40). Then, too, the canary you are about to buy may not be your only pet. Perhaps you already have a dog, a cat, a guinea pig, or a parrot. In that case you have to give some thought to how you introduce the newcomer to the other animals without causing a tragedy. You have to be equally thoughtful if you already have a canary and plan to bring home another pet. But more on all this later (see page 36).

Considerations Before You Buy

For all these reasons you should give careful thought to whether a canary is suitable for you — your particular circumstances and your way of life — before you decide to buy one.

A Single Bird or a Pair

Some people know from the outset that they want a single bird; others toy with the idea of having a pair. If you decide on a pair, start with a male and give it about a year to get used to its new home and to trust you before you add the female. I will talk more about bringing the pair together later (see page 57). As a general rule, I would recommend that you get a single bird if you have a small apartment, are at home a lot, and would like the canary to become attached to you. If you live in a small apartment and work during the day or are away frequently for other reasons, a pair is preferable. The two birds will have each other's company and will not mind your absence as long as they have food and water and plenty of room to move around. If you have a large apartment or a house with a garden, you can keep a number of birds in an aviary.

If it is the song you are interested in, you have to get a single male canary. But that brings us to the next point.

Buying a Singing Bird

Most bird lovers who decide on a canary do so because they want a singing bird. If that is your case, let me give you the following advice: Buy in November or December and choose a young male that was hatched that year and has already learned how to sing. But be sure to obtain a written statement to the effect that the bird can be exchanged if it turns out not to be a singer.

In a well-run pet store, the singers are kept singly in small cages so that you have a chance to listen to them and find one whose voice or repertoire particularly appeals to you (see page 11). Take your time, and listen a while before you make a final decision.

If you want a bird with especially well developed singing abilities (see page 8), consult an expert. Not all canaries have equally pleasant voices, just as not all canaries are yellow. Some have loud and shrill voices that could be more an annoyance than a pleasure in a small apartment. This is particularly true of color canaries that are bred primarily for the brilliance of their plumage. I have already mentioned that breeders now strive to combine melodious song and beautiful coloring.

Considerations Before You Buy

Important Tips for Buying a Bird

When you go to buy a canary, it is good to take along somebody who knows something about birds. Or at least look around and consult friends who already have canaries or other small birds. After all you want to choose a strong, healthy bird, not one that will keel over and die right after you bring it home. If you do have to pick out a bird by yourself, rely on your eyes and your instinct, and watch out for the signs listed below. Generally speaking, you can rely on the advice of a knowledgeable sales person. Most pet stores deal only in healthy birds and try to sell you what you are looking for. But there are exceptions. Take your time when you go to the pet store, and look the birds over carefully. Pretend you are buying a second-hand car. You would not just buy the first one you see. In a way the bird is second hand, too. It has not just hatched. It has been alive for a few months and has already had various experiences.

Watch out especially for the following signs:

Plumage:
• Are the feathers smooth, clean and even?
• Or are they scraggly and dirty?
• Are there bald spots, especially around the head and neck?

Legs:
• Are they clean, and are the horny scales smooth?
• Or are they chapped looking with scales that stick out?
• Are there toes missing or partially missing? Are the nails too long or crooked?

Behavior:
• Is the bird lively? Does it hop around, fly, eat, drink, preen itself, and watch its surroundings with interest?
• Or is it sitting still on its perch, feathers ruffled, eyes closed, breathing heavily, indifferent to what is going on around it?

Digestion:
• Does the bird produce droppings regularly and without apparent effort? Are the feathers around the vent clean?
• Or does it strain unsuccessfully, jerking its tail up and down? Are the feathers around the vent dirty and stuck together?

If you observe even one of the negative signs listed, leave the bird where it is, but bring the problem to the sales person's attention, so that the sick bird is properly attended to.

Where to Buy Your Canary
If you keep my instructions in mind, you can easily examine a bird

and decide whether or not to buy it. This is possible, of course, only if you purchase your canary in a pet store or the pet section of a department store. If you buy it through the mail (and these days there is hardly anything that cannot be ordered through a catalog), you have no chance to inspect it beforehand. You choose from a list, and the bird will be sent to you. You will not know what you are getting until you open the package. Usually you have the right to request a replacement or a refund (be sure to check before you order) if your bird is sick, injured, or dead on arrival. But sometimes you have to return the original shipment, which can be a bother. Or you feel sorry for the sick bird and decide to keep it. If it dies a few days later, you are no longer entitled to a refund or exchange. It is a good idea to get the mailman or delivery man to attest to the condition of the bird upon arrival, especially if it is sick or dead.

Know-How for Buying a Canary

Before you purchase a canary you should familiarize yourself with the bird's anatomy and the vocabulary to describe it. It pays to let the sales person know that you are not totally ignorant about birds. It can be downright embarrassing to be staring at a bird's throat while the sales person is talking about the uropygium, which happens to be located at the opposite end of the bird.

The drawing on page 62 (Figure 27) depicts a made-up bird, combining characteristics of several species.

On the *head* you will find:

Throat	Superciliary lines
Chin	(eye brows)
Lower mandible	Eye lines
Upper mandible	Whisker marks
Forehead	Nares or nostrils
Crown	Ceres
Nape (collar)	Eyes
Auricular area	Eye rings
Lores (median lines)	Ear openings (hidden)

On the *body* you will find:

Back	Breast
Uropygium	Shoulder
(preen gland)	Flank
Vent (cloaca)	Tail
Belly or abdomen	

The *wings* are composed of:

Upper wing	Primaries
Lower wing	Secondaries
Wrist	Scapulars

The *legs* are composed of:

Upper leg	Toes
Lower leg	Claws (nails)
Tarsus	

The *tail* is composed of:

Upper tail coverts	Tail feathers
Under tail coverts	(rectrices)

Male or Female?

Cocks and hens, to use the technical terms, are hard to tell apart for the layman. The song is the only reliable clue. Their appearance differs only in small points. The cocks are usually slightly bigger and stronger than the hens, and the color around the eyes is somewhat brighter, but this is not always the case. When the male is ready to mate (which can happen as early as December), the skin around the cloaca protrudes somewhat. Experts call this a "cone." Females either lack it altogether or have it only in a vestigial form at the rear edge of the cloaca. Ask the owner of the pet store if you cannot tell the sex of a bird.

Keeping Your Bird in a Cage or Aviary

The type and size of your canary's cage depend on the plans you have for your feathered friend. It makes a difference whether you intend to keep the bird in a room or whether you can house him outdoors; whether you are going to keep a single bird or several; or whether you are interested in breeding them. Most novice bird owners start with a single bird.

The Correct Cage

There is a great variety of cages for canaries and other birds on the market, but not all of them are practical or even usable. Keep in mind that the cage must be large enough and appropriate for your bird. Even a single canary needs a cage at least 20 inches (50 cm) long, 12 inches (30 cm) wide, and 16 inches (40 cm) high. Don't forget how small this space is for a creature that in its natural state has the sky for a limit.

You may have seen canaries in very small cages in pet stores or at a breeder's, cages measuring as little as 11½ × 11½ × 7¼ inches (28 × 28 × 18 cm). These are the so-called songbird cages, where male canaries are kept temporarily to develop their songs. In such small cages the birds have nothing to do but sing. In a reasonably large cage or in a room-size or outdoor aviary, the canary is

Figure 3 *Cages with a removable tray can be cleaned quickly and easily.*

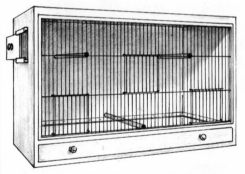

Figure 4 *Box cages with only one side open are good for shy or sick birds.*

able to behave more or less in accordance with its original nature. This may distract him somewhat from singing, but it certainly will not stop him. Surely you would rather have a bird that will stay healthy and live for several years, though he may sing a little less, than one that warbles from dawn to dusk only to sicken and die

19

after a couple of years from lack of exercise.

So much for the size of the cage. In addition to being large enough, the cage should also be practical — for the bird as well as for you. The bird must be able to hop around properly and at least flap around in the cage if flying is impossible. He must be able to get at his food, water, and bathtub easily. Make sure there is no possibility for him to get stuck or squeezed anywhere. And you yourself should be able to clean and move the cage without difficulty. As I have already mentioned, cages of various designs are available. But not all of them are practical. Some features are merely ornamental, which your bird will not appreciate at all. On the contrary, ornament may add to his oppression. Shiny or white bars may look attractive, but you may hardly be able to see the bird behind all the glitter. Darker bars with a matte finish are easier on the eye and give you a better view. It goes without saying that the bars must be set close enough that the canary cannot slip between them. He should not even be able to stick his head through the bars, because pulling it back against the growth of the feathers may be problematical, and he might strangle in the process (Figure 6).

Make sure that the cage has a tray above the floor that pulls out easily, and that there is a flap that closes over the opening between the tray and the floor. If there is no such flap or no floor below the tray, the bird can escape while you are cleaning the cage. The lower part of the cage should be covered all around with glass, plastic, or wood to a height of four to five inches. This prevents sand, food, or

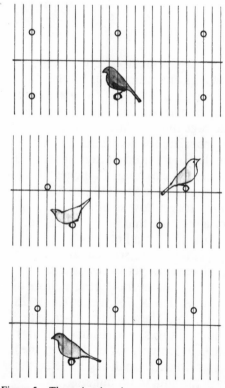

Figure 5 *These sketches show various ways of placing perches in the cage.*

droppings from spilling. All doors to the cage must shut tightly and securely so that they will not open accidentally.

In addition to cages which have bars all around there are also the so-called box cages. These have bars only in front; the rest of the cage consists of wood. This type of cage is suitable for acclimatizing shy birds and for isolating sick birds.

If you have any chance to expose your canary to fresh air and sunlight, do so by all means. You can take his cage to a balcony, patio, porch, or backyard. But never place it in the hot noon or afternoon sun or in a windy or drafty location. Half sun, half shade is best, as under a tree, for example. But watch out for cats. If you drape a cloth over the top and sides of the cage, the bird will be protected from drafts.

Indoor Aviaries as Part of the Living Room

An aviary is preferable to a cage. An aviary is a cage large enough for a bird to fly freely in it. You can also keep several canaries in it or combine canaries and other types of granivorous birds (see page 29). Basically the same rules apply to an aviary as to a small cage. However, the grating usually consists of wire mesh with spaces of about ½ inch rather than bars. A

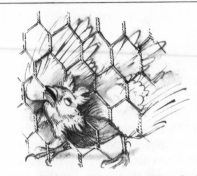

Figure 6 *The cage grating can turn into a death trap if the holes are large enough to let the bird stick his head out but too small to let him pull it back in.*

Figure 7 *With a small enough mesh such disasters can be prevented.*

mesh with a plastic coating is desirable because birds are not as likely to injure themselves as they are if they fly against galvanized wire mesh. Indoor as well as outdoor aviaries are commercially available (see page 20). But you can also construct them yourself and end up with a custom-built product that suits your particular setup.

Small, hinged wire doors will not do for an aviary. After all, you must be able to enter the aviary to clean it or check on nesting boxes or catch injured and sick birds. The aviary must therefore be equipped with a proper door, but this door should not be larger than necessary. If several birds live in an aviary and flutter about nervously when someone enters, one or more of them might flit out the door in the general commotion. The door should be as narrow as possible and located on the side opposite from the main light source, because birds tend to fly toward the light.

When you outfit an aviary, you can give more rein to your imagination than when you equip a cage. Branches and twigs of varying size afford the birds a chance to use their feet and toes. The standard perches in cages measure ½ inch in diameter and are made of hardwood or grooved plastic. Every landing is a jolt for the bird, and he has to use the same toe grip over and over again. This can, in the long run, lead to foot diseases. Even if you keep your bird in a cage, it is a good idea to add sticks of varying sizes to the standard perches. In your aviary you should use nothing but natural branches from all kinds of trees and replace them frequently. They get dirty more quickly than smooth, polished bars, and they are not easy to clean. But it is well worth taking this extra trouble.

Aviaries on Balconies or in the Backyard

I mentioned in my discussion of cages that canaries should be exposed to the open air whenever possible. A bird that can choose its own favorite spots in an outdoor aviary is better off than a bird that lives indoors. The rules for an indoor aviary apply to the outdoor one too. But while the birds are protected inside, they are subject to enemy attacks outdoors. Cats, marten, weasels, rats, and owls will try to enter the aviary at night. Rats and mice may dig their way in if the aviary is placed on the ground. Ideally it should be built on a concrete foundation three feet deep.

If you find rodent holes in the ground, you can set out traps or poison outside the aviary. There is little you can do against cats and owls. The best protection against these nighttime invaders is to have two layers of wire mesh, separated by a space of three to four inches. This costs money, of course, and it obstructs the view into the aviary somewhat. Another method for keeping enemies out is to run a low-voltage electric wire around the outside of the aviary at the top and bottom. Be sure this wire does not come in contact with the wire mesh. If a predator touches the electric wire, it will receive a shock not strong enough to hurt it but sufficient to drive it away. (Electric fences around cattle pastures work on the same principle.)

Your outdoor aviary should be protected from winds and heavy rains. There is no harm if rain occasionally enters it, as long as the birds have a dry spot to retire to. Your setup is close to ideal if about one-quarter to one-third of the aviary is protected by a waterproof roof and this section is also tightly closed in with stone, wood, or plastic. This provides the birds with a dry, protected corner they can retreat to in bad weather. If the aviary is attached to your house, this protected area usually adjoins the wall of the house. This kind of arrangement may give you the extra benefit of looking out into the aviary from your living-room window and observing the birds without upsetting them.

You can also plant bushes and trees in an outdoor aviary. Canaries like to eat buds and other parts of plants in addition to their usual diet of grain and seeds (see page 41). As long as the aviary is spacious enough and not overpopulated with canaries and other granivorous birds (especially parakeets and small parrots), there will be no noticeable damage to your plants. Evergreens, hard-leafed plants, conifers, willows, birches, poplars, and fruit trees can be planted in aviaries. If the canaries have access to a fully enclosed space with heating and artificial light, they can be left outdoors year round. Once used to the outdoors, canaries are quite hardy and can tolerate temperatures a few degrees below freezing.

You can also connect your aviary to a room inside the house or to an indoor aviary by means of a window or hatch. But birds do not like to fly through small hatches. If you use a hatch, you should provide a small landing board on either side so that the birds can enter and depart "on foot."

Birds that have access to the outdoors all year or as long as the weather is suitable are healthier and livelier than their fellows who spend all their time indoors.

Necessary Supplies

I have already mentioned perches in my remarks on outfitting indoor aviaries and briefly discussed the drawbacks of artificial perches (see page 22). The uniform diameter of commercially available perches allows for only one type of toe hold, and every landing represents a small shock to the

Keeping Your Bird in a Cage or Aviary

Figure 8 *Perches should be thick enough to keep the bird's claws from going all the way around. Left: correct; right: incorrect.*

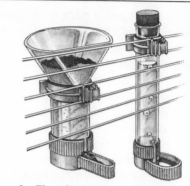

Figure 9 *These food and water containers are filled from the top and release their contents at the bottom. Check every day to see that they are functioning properly.*

bird's system because the perch lacks elasticity. Natural perches give when the bird lands. The different thicknesses of branches and twigs and their differing degrees of solidity provide your canary with the occasion to exercise foot and toe muscles and keep its feet limber and healthy. Aviaries are a perfect place for natural perches. Choose small limbs from fruit trees, poplars, ash, willows, spruce, elderberry, etc., with as many branches and twigs as possible.

But even if you keep your bird in a cage, you should remove the perches and replace them with sticks. Perches, both natural and artificial, should be thick enough so that the bird's toes cannot reach around them completely, and they should be placed at varied heights and locations in the cage.

Choose the food and water containers carefully. You can buy tube-shaped water dispensers with a drinking basin at the bottom. The basin should be just large enough for the bird to reach the water with its beak. The dispensers vary in size,

some holding enough water for a single day, others enough for several days. These latter should be used only on occasions when you have to leave the bird alone for more than one day. Ordinarily it must get fresh water daily. The dispensers are fastened to the cage by squeezing the appropriate part between the bars (Figure 9) from the inside or the outside. If you have an aviary, you will probably have to tie the container to the mesh with wire to make sure that it will stay in place.

Similar dispensers are available for dry bird food. Here, too, you can pour a fair amount of food into the container, and a small portion is available at the bottom, continually replenished as the bird eats. Be sure, before you buy a dispenser of this type, that it is the right size for the bird food

24

mixture you use. If the seeds are too small, they will all run out the bottom at once. If they are too large, they will get stuck, and your bird will have to go hungry in plain sight of the food.

Soft food is best offered in plain china bowls that are easily cleaned. Plastic gets scratched quickly and dirt gets stuck in seams and cracks. You can also buy special containers for soft food that snap between two bars of the cage. Squeeze greens and fruit between the bars where the bird can reach them easily from a perch, or suspend them from the top of the cage speared on a wooden skewer. If you have an aviary, you can stick fruit and greens in the wire mesh or spear pieces of apple, for instance, on the ends of twigs. If a number of birds live in one aviary, they must have several food and water dishes at appropriate spots.

Figure 10   *This type of plastic feeder is available in many colors and is suitable for both water and food.*

Nearly all birds love to take baths and do so often. Canaries are no exception. Pet stores sell small "bath houses" which are closed in on all but one side and thus prevent the water

from squirting all over in the course of this often exuberant exercise. You may want to equip your bird with such a bath house, particularly if its cage is in your living room. If you don't mind an occasional soaking of your furniture, you can give your bird an earthenware flowerpot saucer or some similar dish to bathe in. But make sure that the bottom of the dish is not too smooth and the water in it comes up no higher than the feathers on the bird's belly. A canary is not a duck. He cannot swim and therefore likes to bathe in shallow puddles. He also needs a firm footing while he is splashing about. If he keeps slipping, he will become unsure of himself and nervous. Therefore be sure that the bottom of the bathtub is fairly rough. If necessary you can place a piece of foam rubber in the bottom.

Figure 11   *Bird baths should have rough bottoms so that birds will not slip on them.*

Keeping Your Bird in a Cage or Aviary

Finally, you can buy special clamps to hold calcium stones and racks for greens.

You should also give some thought to lighting. If your cage or aviary gets daylight directly from a window facing south, you have an ideal situation. The birds should not be exposed to direct sunlight for any length of time. If the room does not get sufficient daylight, you will have to supply artificial lighting. True Lite Duro Test light tubes are far better than normal light bulbs or fluorescent lighting. In addition to light, they give off ultraviolet and infrared rays, which are important to keep the birds healthy. These tubes come in 20, 30, 40, and 65 watt strengths and in different lengths. They are expensive, but they are well worth their price.

Care and Maintenance

You probably don't like to eat off dirty plates. Neither does your bird. Cleanliness is of the utmost importance in keeping birds. Clean all containers *before* feeding and watering your bird. Change the drinking water whenever it gets contaminated with food or droppings but at least twice a day.

The following is a list of what you need to do for your bird and how often.

Daily:
Give food and fresh drinking water; replace bath water; clean water dispenser and drinking basin; remove leftover food; clean the floor of the cage. You should also check daily to make sure that water tubes and food tubes are in proper working order and fastened securely, that the doors to the cage shut tightly, that no decaying bits of food are lodged in cracks or grooves. Observe the bird carefully for signs of unusual behavior, illness (see page 46), or injury.

Weekly:
Clean the cage or aviary, including all perches both artificial and natural; wash all food, water, and bath dishes thoroughly; replace sand in the bottom of the cage; clean the floor of the aviary thoroughly — if it consists of earth, rake it, or if it is made up of flag stones, cement, etc., hose it down.

Monthly:
Check birds for vermin (are they scratching a lot?); check toe nails for length; check aviary for leaks.

About four times annually:
Disinfect cage, aviary, any supplies thoroughly (e.g., with Lysol); replace natural branches and twigs with new ones; fork up the soil in an outdoor aviary.

◁ Plate 4 *Above, left to right: Pastel golden agate,*
pale yellow, bright copper red, bright orange red,
pale silver brown.
Below: Color varieties from a cross between a
black finch and a canary.

A Canary Together with Other Birds

Is your new canary going to live with other birds already established in your indoor or outdoor aviary? As a rule, canaries live harmoniously with other kinds of birds without creating any problem. It is best to combine canaries with granivorous birds of similar size. Canaries get along well with parakeets, ornamental finches, as well as other finches, and several types of doves. Other birds may get along well with each other, too, but it is a good idea to check with the breeder before you buy.

You should keep in mind a few basic rules when you add a new bird to a group of already established ones. The birds that have lived in the aviary for some time have adjusted to their environment and know their way around. They know where to find food and water, they claim certain perches for resting and sleeping, and (this holds especially true for pairs of birds) they establish their own territories.

A new bird is unaware of all this when he joins the group. His surroundings as well as his new companions are unknown to him. He is frightened and shy; he has to learn where food and water are available; and he has to find a perch for himself.

But generally he will not be able to establish himself on his own because the other birds will rouse him and chase him as soon as he enters their territories or is about to occupy one of their perches. In a natural environment this presents no grave problem. The bird will flee when chased until it eventually finds a spot that is not contested.

But within the limited world of an aviary he cannot get away. He will be physically attacked and chased until he cowers exhausted in the farthest corner of the aviary. It is hard to believe how quickly an otherwise peaceful bird can kill a bird he does not take to. He may not even resort to attacking the newcomer with beak, wings, and legs. He can simply threaten and frighten him so much that the newcomer will not dare approach the food and will die after a few days from exhaustion and hunger.

This is why you cannot introduce a new bird into a group of already established ones and expect that all will be well. This is especially true during mating season if a pair of canaries is already living in the aviary, or if other kinds of birds have established a breeding territory there. There is no absolutely safe rule for introducing a canary to birds already living in an aviary. But there are some precautions you can take.

• Place the newcomer in a small cage

29

Keeping Your Bird in a Cage or Aviary

and put the cage inside the aviary for a few days. In this sanctuary the bird has a chance to become familiar with his new environment. The established birds can in turn get accustomed to him without hurting him. When he is later released from the cage, everyone will "know" each other, and there will probably be less reason for aggression.
• Or you can catch the birds already living in the aviary, house them somewhere else temporarily, and allow the newcomer a few days by himself to familiarize himself with his new home. Then you return the other birds to the aviary. But whatever you do, be on the constant alert during the first few days so that you can intervene quickly in a struggle.

Birds fight not just when a newcomer joins an established group. Sometimes after a long time of peaceful coexistence trouble will start in a communal aviary. The usual cause is that two birds have paired and are defending their breeding territory. If you want to keep the other birds out of danger and protect the brood that may result, you have to give the cage or aviary over to the mating pair and remove the other birds. After the mating season is over and the young have become independent, you can bring everybody together again.

The Bird in His New Home

The Trip Home

When you have made your selection and bought the bird it will be handed to you in a small cardboard box with air holes. This is the usual procedure. Be sure the bird is not placed in a plastic or paper bag. In a plastic bag it will overheat or suffocate; in a paper bag it may get crushed or escape. Now take it home carefully.

Basic Rules for Acclimatizing the Bird

The First Hours and Days at Home

When you get home, everything should be ready for the new arrival. The cage (see page 19) or aviary (see page 21) must be completely equipped

Figure 12 *First outing. Using the open door of his cage as his base, the canary investigates the immediate surroundings of his cage.*

and food and water set out, so that the bird can be released as quickly as possible from the confinement of its cardboard prison. Of course you will previously have considered and decided what the most suitable place for the bird will be. The proximity of radios or a television set, as well as of radiators, is undesirable. Choose a quiet, bright, and draft-free spot.

Birds are primarily vision-oriented. They quickly register everything new around them, especially an environment that is totally unfamiliar and therefore threatening. If you have to reach into the aviary and adjust things at this point, you will frighten the bird even more. It might happen that the bird associates its terror with you, and this first bad impression may interfere in the process of getting acquainted.

Open the transport container gently and hold it up against the cage opening so that there is no crack through which the bird can escape. Since birds are attracted to light, your canary will hop out of the box on his own. If your bird is going to live in an aviary, place the box in the aviary, open it carefully, and leave. You can remove the box later when the bird has had a chance to get acquainted with his new home. If the aviary is already occupied, you have to take special measures, as described on page 29.

If you use an aviary, especially an

The Bird in His New Home

outdoor aviary, it is important to place the bird in his new surroundings as early in the day as possible. He has to have time to orient himself before dark. Never grab your bird from the transport box. No bird likes to be handled by a stranger.

When the canary is safely inside his new cage, close the cage door slowly, and step back a few feet. Naturally you will be curious to see what the bird does, but hold back and allow him to get acquainted with the cage without you hovering over him at this difficult moment. Move around slowly and quietly. You may talk to him in a soft and soothing voice from a distance while he still hops nervously from perch to perch. When he fluffs up and starts preening himself, it is a sign that he is beginning to relax. Once he starts feeding and drinking, the worst is over.

During the first few days of acclimatization a cloth should be draped over the top and back of the cage. This will add to the bird's sense of security.

Canaries have lived in domesticity for centuries, and chances are that your bird will adjust quickly to his new life. After two to three weeks, you can let your little friend fly freely in the house, but make sure all windows and doors are shut. Open the cage door, and he will come out of his

own accord. Later, when he gets hungry, he will return on his own. But don't rush him into the venture. Give him ample time to get used to the cage and to accept it as a place of safety and a source of food and shelter.

First Free Flights Indoors

I have already said when you can first let your canary fly free and that you must be careful not to leave doors and windows open. Birds, like moths, are drawn to light. But when they start out they do not know that there is a hard, transparent barrier between the

Figure 13 *Only a bird that is allowed to fly outside its cage occasionally will stay healthy and happy.*

room and the light outside. Almost inevitably your canary will collide with a window. If his momentum is not too great when he crashes, he will simply

The Bird in His New Home

slide down the glass and land on the window sill somewhat stunned. After he has gone through this a few times, he will learn to recognize the strange barrier and avoid it. If he crashes hard against the window, he may sustain a concussion, and you must place him in a dark, quiet place. If there is no cerebral hemorrhage, he will recover in a few hours. If the impact is very great, he may break his neck and die instantly.

To prevent such accidents, you should draw the curtains or close the blinds whenever you let the bird fly free, whenever you handle sick or injured birds, and at any other time when birds might escape from the cage or aviary.

One very good solution is to place screens on the inside of windows in the room where the birds are. Then you can air the room whenever you want, whether the birds are in the cage or outside. Other dangers to free-flying birds are mentioned in the list of dangers on page 35. You should in any case provide perches wherever you let your bird fly. Place newspapers underneath them, and the cleaning up after the bird will be much easier. One final piece of advice: Do not provide food or water outside the cage. This way the bird will return to his cage of his own free will when he gets hungry or thirsty.

Danger, Indoors and Out

You and your family will get much enjoyment from a free-flying canary; and the bird, too, will be happy to have freedom of movement, at least intermittently. But the pleasure will soon turn sour if the bird unsuspectingly tries to settle on a hot toaster or stove and burns his feet. In one quirk accident a canary sat on a toaster, pecked at some crumbs between the wires, received a shock, and died instantly.

Hot objects and electrical appliances are not the only dangers. Smooth surfaces offer a precarious foothold. If your bird flies free, most of his landing places will be more or less slippery, and he may end up in a spot not at all of his choosing, e.g., between a piece of furniture and the wall, where he will hang like a mountain climber in a crevice of a glacier. His only hope is that you will find him in time.

A bouquet of flowers adds a lovely touch to a room. But if you remove the wilted flowers and leave the vase with water still in it, the canary may land on it, try to drink, fall in, and drown.

A room where a bird flies at large should be as free as possible of such traps. The less furniture the better. It is easier to keep clean that way, too. If

The Bird in His New Home

a canary is very tame, he will want to stay as close as possible to you, and you must take extra care when entering or leaving a room not to catch the bird in a door and not to step on him. Or you might accidentally sit on him while he is picking up a tiny crumb from your chair or sofa. I once had a tame chickadee that had chosen a hat-rack by the door as his favorite sleeping place. It would sit there, all fluffed up, beak tucked under the wing, and sleep — until one evening a guest vigorously tossed his hat up on the stand.

It is a good idea to tell visitors that there is a bird flying free in your home. People generally find it startling or even frightening to have a bird fly at them unexpectedly, and someone might react in a manner harmful to the bird.

Once you know your bird fairly well, you will be able to anticipate what frightens him. He may be thrown into a minor panic by a stranger (particularly if the person is wearing bright colors), by a strange animal, or even at the sight of a new umbrella. He will then flutter around his cage all adither. If this happens, cover the cage with a cloth, so that he can calm down again.

A room generally contains more traps and causes for accidents than an indoor or outdoor aviary. Outdoors, the animals mentioned on page 22 represent a danger, as do rusty nails, pieces of sharp wire, etc. Check everything out at least twice a year. The wear and tear of time will show up where you least expect it. Wires holding different parts of the aviary together rust, wood rots, leaves and dirt collect on the roof, and someday the whole aviary might collapse. Frost makes foundations heave or cracks them, thus creating access for rodents. A tree nearby may be rotten and drop a heavy limb on the aviary in a storm. Winter brings additional dangers with it. Snow will accumulate on the roof. Be sure there is enough support so that it will not collapse.

I have prepared a list of possible dangers to look out for. I tried to be as thorough as possible, but remember, there is always something one does not anticipate.

Figure 14 *The windowpane as bird trap: If a canary flies into an unprotected window he can fracture his neck or skull.*

34

The Bird in His New Home

List of Dangers

Danger	Effect	Danger	Effect
Draft from open doors and windows	Colds	Threads and thin strings	Getting caught in a loop and strangling
Open drawers, closets	Suffocation	Spaces between walls and furniture	Sliding between and getting stuck
Steam from cooking	Internal illnesses		
Hot pots, dishes with hot liquids	Burns, drowning	Hard flooring	Nestlings may fall hard and break bones
Chemical cleaners	Poisoning	Wrong size wire mesh or bars too far apart	Getting head stuck. Outdoors: entry of predators
Open bathroom door	Slipping and drowning		
Candle light	Burns	Wires too fine	Injuries to toes and head
Windows and glass doors	Concussion, broken skull or neck	Perches too thin	Overgrowth of nails
Doors	Getting caught and squashed	Wire mesh rusting through	Escape
Open windows and doors	Escape outdoors	Open pipes, ducts	Sliding in, suffocating
Stove tops, radiators, electrical appliances	Burns	Ends of wire, nails, splinters, etc.	Pricks and cuts
Electrical cords and outlets	Electrocution	Loose perches	Falls, fractures
Pitchers, vases, water buckets, basins, etc.	Slipping in and drowning	Snow on aviary roof	Roof collapsing and burying birds
Loose-weave materials	Catching of claws, strangling	Feet	Crushing underfoot

Plate 5 *These studies by master photographer* ▷
*Hans Reinhard show a bright orange Roller in
flight.*

Watch Out for Other Pets

Birds, especially small ones, have an inborn fear of large birds as well as of just about any fur-bearing animal. This makes sense since their natural predators, dogs, cats, weasels, foxes, etc., are furry. Your canary has no way of telling that your dog is well trained and represents no danger whatsoever. He will be frightened. Even though canaries have lost some of their native shyness in the centuries of their domestication, they have not lost all their instincts. So don't let your dog near the cage when the canary has barely gotten settled. This would practically give the bird a heart attack. Don't pay any attention to pictures you may have seen in pet magazines that show a canary or a parakeet perched on the head of a cat or dog. It may occasionally happen that a bird and a predator become friends, but this is the result of long and careful training. You can never be sure that the peace will last and that the cat or dog will be able to stay in control of his instincts. After all, they are hunters who respond automatically to the fluttering or hopping of a prey that has gotten trapped.

A cat may get so used to a canary hopping around in its cage that he pays no attention to it. But if the bird flies around the room and perhaps lands in front of the cat's nose, the old hunting instinct may be activated, and that will be the end of the bird. Watch birds and other pets carefully, particularly at the beginning. Allow them to get acquainted slowly and from a safe distance. Never leave them alone in a room unsupervised.

Cats and dogs are not the only pets that represent a danger. Rabbits, guinea pigs, hamsters, or squirrels can also be a threat. Not that these animals are interested in the canary as food. They would not kill it to eat it, but they might attack it because it has invaded their territory. I once watched a tame male rabbit almost kill a jackdaw I had placed in the aviary where the rabbit lived. I had thought the bird would stay on the perches up in the air. But after a while it flew to the ground, and the rabbit set about belaboring it with teeth and paws so fast I hardly had time to intervene.

Let us assume your dog and canary are good friends. Such friendships between disparate creatures do exist. But dangers are still inherent in the different behavioral patterns of birds and dogs. A dog wanting to play will, for instance, paw at his friend. This is fine as long as the playmate is another dog or a human being. But what if it is a small canary? The dog doesn't have to be a Saint Bernard for the results to be disastrous. If you have had the dog

36

for some time and the bird is a newcomer, the dog will of course be jealous because of the attention you pay to the bird. Don't aggravate the situation by telling the dog how nice the bird is. Instead, tell him to leave the bird alone in the same firm voice you used to tell him that the sofa is off limits.

Small mammals and cats are not as easily trained as dogs. With them, you must watch out all the more carefully to prevent disasters.

If Your Bird Escapes

One fall morning I went out to my garden and found a bright orange canary chirping up at me from the ground. I went to get my bird net and caught him. It was sheer chance that I caught him rather than a roaming cat, a weasel, or some bird of prey. A discouragingly large number of canaries escape and meet with death. Canaries can live up to about ten years if they don't escape or meet with some fatal accident.

Unfortunately we often do not learn, until sad experience teaches us, how to protect birds from disaster. If your bird escapes, it is indeed a disaster. His bright coloring makes him an easy prey for any hunter, both four-footed and avian. It is no accident that albinos (animals that are partially or entirely white as a result of a chance mutation) do not survive long in the wild. A yellow or red canary is no better off. In addition, it has lost the ability to find food on its own. In summertime it may be able to survive, but when fall comes, it will starve to death.

After escaping through an open door or window, the bird will at first be totally frightened by his unfamiliar surroundings. Usually he will fly upward and sit in a tree out of reach from the ground. Try to keep him in sight. If you are lucky, he will not go far, but a flock of sparrows, a gust of wind, or something else may scare him and he will be gone for good.

If the bird stays close for a few hours, you may be lucky and get him back. Place his cage on the window sill, on the balcony, or in the garden, and put some clearly visible food around it and inside it. If the bird gets hungry, he may return to his cage.

If your bird escapes from an outdoor aviary, the situation is different. He is already somewhat familiar with the new environment and is likely to stick around. He will probably soon perch on the aviary, ready to return to his familiar grounds and his food. If possible, move the other birds out of the aviary, open the doors wide, and chances are the escapee will fly in of his own accord.

The Bird in His New Home

If a very tame bird has escaped, he will probably return to you even outside. But he will be shier than in his usual surroundings, and you should have your bird net (you should have one anyway to catch birds you want to move out of the aviary) ready to plunk over him. With the help of a bird net you can even catch a bird in the air, though that trick requires a bit of practice.

Traveling with Your Bird

If you want to go on a trip, you can do one of two things: You can take your canary along, or you can leave it at home. You may prefer to take it along, but the bird is no doubt happier at home. It is most comfortable where it knows its way around. Still, canaries are not as fussy and shy as some other types of pet birds. If you have a canary that is used to living by itself in a cage, you can take it along without doing it any harm. Cover the cage completely with a light cloth so that the bird is safe from drafts. Seeing the scenery flit by in a moving car is no treat for your canary. It will simply upset him and make him nervous. A thin cloth will let enough light through so that the bird can see his food, and he stays calmer if he is in the dark. But you must be sure to stop at least every couple of hours, remove the cloth, and let the bird eat and drink in peace.

If you cross a border, the customs official will usually not be too interested in your canary. But there are state and federal laws governing the transport and import of birds. Be sure you know the applicable laws. Your local U.S. Department of Agriculture can supply you with all necessary information. The country you wish to enter may have regulations, too, and you should inquire about them beforehand at the consulate in question.

If you are going to leave your bird at home, you have to make appropriate arrangements. The person who will look after your canary should be as reliable as your babysitter. The caretaker has to know your bird's habits, such as when it is usually fed and under what conditions it flies free. If you are gone only for a day or two, your canary will manage by itself. Just make sure there is enough food and water available for the period of your absence and that the bird will be able to get at it (see page 24).

You should not take birds that are used to living in an aviary on a trip. They react much more negatively to changes in their surroundings than birds kept in cages. Aviaries are too big to fit into cars, and transplanting birds to cages when they are not used to them is a traumatic experience for them. You will therefore have to get someone to look after them if you go away on a vacation.

Canary Nutrition

Food and Feeding

Most animals living in captivity do not get the varied diet they would enjoy in their natural habitat. This is especially true of birds which, thanks to their ability to fly, have access to all kinds of food sources. However, if you are willing to go to some trouble and give some attention to the nutritional needs of your canary, you will find ways to offer him a varied and healthy diet. Keep in mind:

- Food in its natural, unadulterated state is best.
- The more varied the diet, the healthier the bird.
- The food should be as fresh as possible.

Tame birds that fly free in your house often like to join you at mealtime. There is nothing wrong with that. A bird will rarely eat something that is bad for it. Even if your bird occasionally snitches a few grains of salt or a beak full of butter or salad dressing, there is no need to worry. However, if he gets used to human food and prefers it to his own, you have to watch out. This predilection can lead to obesity and digestive problems.

General Nutritional Needs

Canaries eat primarily grains and seeds, but they also need fresh foods like sprouts, lettuce, chickweed, fruit, and young shoots and buds from fruit trees. A cuttlebone is essential for supplying calcium and other minerals. And, of course, water for drinking must be available.

Dry Bird Food

The main diet should consist of a variety of grains and seeds. Many commercial mixes designed for canaries are available. Each bird has his own likes and dislikes. If you have several birds in an aviary you may want to offer different seeds in separate containers, particularly at the beginning when you are figuring out preferences. You avoid waste in this way because a lot of food gets spilled when the birds pick through the mixture in search of their favorite seeds. Offer separate bowls of different seeds. You will soon notice which kinds are consistently refused. Once you know your birds' tastes you can switch to a commercial mix that does not include seeds your birds don't like. For a single bird, a ready mix is very convenient. A typical mix consists of canary, rape, niger, and smaller quantities of hemp, linseed, lettuce, and poppy seeds.

Sprouts

Like all finches, canaries like not only dry seeds but also sprouted ones.

Canary Nutrition

Sprouts are very healthy, but they must be prepared with care. Place one day's ration of mixed seeds in a small plastic sieve and suspend it in a jar of water so that all the seeds are submerged. After twelve hours remove the sieve with the seeds, rinse with clean, cold water, and suspend again in fresh water. Repeat after twelve hours, but this time place seeds above water and cover. In about twenty-four hours the seeds will begin to sprout. Rinse a third time with cold water, then place on a towel to draw out excess moisture, and the sprouts are ready. Feed them to the birds in a shallow bowl. Because sprouts spoil easily, particularly if packed too tightly, examine them frequently and throw them out if they smell bad or show mold. But sprouts are high in vitamins, and you should periodically go to the trouble of making them for your birds.

Fruit and Greens

In addition to mixed bird seed you should regularly offer greens and/or fruit. Birds are fond of chickweed, lettuce, spinach, and dandelion greens. But if you gather the greens yourself on walks, avoid areas that may have been sprayed. Herbicides and pesticides can be fatal to your birds. Greens from your own garden or an-other organic source are best. If you must buy them in a supermarket, be sure to wash and dry them thoroughly. The same goes for fruit. Offer fresh food in small quantities; too much causes diarrhea. In the winter, fruit is a good substitute for greens. Canaries also like buds and shoots from deciduous trees.

Soft Food (Rearing and Conditioning Food)

In addition to seeds, canaries enjoy soft food. They will feed it to their young (see page 61), and they will eat it themselves year round. It is particularly good for them during molting, because it is high in protein.

You can buy this soft food ready made in pet stores. Feed it in separate bowls, not mixed in with the bird seed.

Vitamins, Minerals, and Trace Elements

Birds that get greens, fruit, sprouts, and soft food in addition to bird seed most of the year will not usually need vitamins, minerals, or trace elements. But there is no harm in occasionally giving them vitamin supplements that are available at pet stores. Excess vitamins are automatically eliminated

Canary Nutrition

by the body. Unlike sprouts, greens, etc., vitamins should be mixed in with the bird seed or added to the drinking water. Minerals and trace elements can be supplied in the form of sepia (cuttlebone) or crushed egg shells which, if they are not boiled, should be baked in the oven.

Daily Food Rations

The basic rule is that the daily amount of food that a small bird needs is equal to about one third of his body weight. Birds should be fed twice a day. The exact amount depends on a number of factors. Birds will eat less if the food is very high in calories or if they sit in small cages and have little exercise. If they move about a lot or if they are laying eggs or raising young, they will eat more. Birds that are outside and are exposed to changes in weather also need more than those that live inside in constant temperatures.

Watch your canary. If he has finished his morning ration soon after feeding time and keeps hunting for more, the serving was too skimpy. If there is still food left in the dish by the time of the second feeding, you can cut back some.

If your canary suddenly eats twice or only half the usual amount, this is not necessarily a cause for alarm.

Figure 15 *This is the way a canary drinks. First, he scoops the water up in his beak; then he lifts his head and lets the water run down into his throat.*

Other signs are more reliable symptoms of illness (see page 46). No bird is totally consistent in his eating habits. I have already mentioned egg laying and raising of young as causes for increased food intake. During molting (see page 51), too, birds need more and especially varied food. Since molting takes place in the summer this usually presents no problem.

Water for Drinking and Bathing

It goes without saying that your canary needs water to drink. Don't give him chlorinated water fresh from the tap. Let it stand for a few hours or, even better, boil it and let it cool to room temperature. If you use a water dispenser (see page 24) that holds enough water for several days, don't let the water sit until it forms scum or grows algae. Change the water every day, unless you are absent for a couple of days. If you use drinking bowls, the water should be changed at least twice a day or whenever it gets contaminated by droppings or scraps of food. The bath water must always be separate from the drinking water. Of course, you cannot keep your bird from taking an occasional drink from his bathtub, but generally he will prefer the clean drinking water. Still, the bath water should be replaced every day. For the bath, too, use water that has been allowed to stand for a while at room temperature.

Is Your Canary Too Fat or Too Thin?

Birds living in the wild spend most of their time preening themselves and looking for food. During the breeding season they also have to take care of the young. Their metabolic rate is high; they use up a lot of energy and must replenish it with a constant intake of food. They cannot go long without food, because if they become weak, they easily succumb to predators, rivals, or bad weather.

Birds living in a natural habitat spend a lot of time and energy in the search for food. Caged birds have much less exercise. The food bowl is only a hop or two from the perch. Even in a fair sized aviary it doesn't take much energy to get to the food. The result of all this is that caged birds tend to obesity. Lack of activity is one cause; one-sided or incorrect diet is another. Feed your canary small amounts at a time but regularly, and give him the opportunity to fly freely as often as you can.

How can you tell whether your bird is too fat or too thin? It is not as easy as it is with a dog. If your dachshund is as wide as he is long, you know that he is too fat. If you can count his ribs, he is too thin. You can't see a bird's ribs because he is covered all over with feathers. To tell what shape he is in, you have to take him in your hand and feel his breast, i.e., the flying muscles, and his breastbone. If the bone sticks out like a ridge in the middle, the bird is too thin. If you cannot feel the bone because the muscles bulge out on either side, the

Figure 16 *The underbelly of your canary can tell you whether you are feeding him correctly. Left: Too thin — the breastbone (sternum) protrudes sharply. Right: Too fat — the sternum is almost completely covered by the breast muscles.*

Canary Nutrition

bird is too fat (Figure 16). The second condition is harder to tell.

If the emaciation is not due to illness, you should give the bird more — and more varied — food. If you have an obese bird, stop feeding him seeds that are high in fat, such as niger and hemp, and give him more fruit and greens instead. But don't put him on an extreme reducing diet. If you were to impose one day of fasting a week on your bird, his health would suffer severely.

Diseases of Canaries

General Symptoms and What to Do

In nature you will seldom come across a sick bird. If he is not in top shape, he will be an easy victim for his enemies. The law of nature is that only the strong and healthy survive. If you find a few feathers and delicate bones, you can guess what happened, but you get no clue what illness might have triggered it.

If you check your pet bird daily, you will know right away when it gets sick. Since there are no enemies around to take advantage of the bird's weakened condition, the patient can often be saved if the right treatment is initiated in time.

Figure 17 *When a canary is sick, he perches more in a lying than in a sitting position, and his eyes are half closed.*

But I would advise you not to experiment with home remedies unless you have a lot of experience in handling sick birds. You will probably do more harm than good. Get in touch with a veterinarian as soon as you can, and follow his instructions.

A sick bird sits still with his feathers all fluffed up (Figure 17). His eyes are half closed, and he often breathes with difficulty. He shows little or no interest in his surroundings. The vent is often dirty, and he has trouble passing stool. The bird is lethargic and stops eating, drinking, and singing. These are usually signs of internal illness.

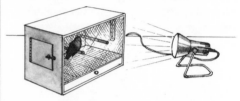

Figure 18 *A special small cage for the sick bird: A thermometer is attached to the wall, and an infrared lamp supplies healing warmth.*

External injuries, such as broken wings or legs, seem to bother a bird much less. Often you can tell that something is amiss only by seeing or feeling the broken bone.

If the sick or injured bird is living with other birds in an aviary or by itself in a large cage, it must first be moved to a smaller cage that serves as an infirmary (Figure 18). Here it needs warmth above all. It is best to use an infrared light, because it is no strain on the eyes. But in a pinch, a normal forty-watt bulb will do too. The temperature in the cage should be about 85°F (30°C) but never above 90°F (32°C). Be sure you protect the bird

Diseases of Canaries

from drafts, but remember that a closed space easily overheats. As the bird starts getting better you can lower the temperature gradually. Don't return the bird to the aviary too soon, or it is bound to suffer a relapse.

A First Aid Kit for Birds

You should have a first-aid kit readily available for emergencies, and it should contain at least the following items:

Heat lamp (infrared)
Antibiotics for bacterial infections, e.g., aureomycin, terramycin, possibly penicillin
Topical *powders* and *ointments* for external wounds
Coagulant cotton swabs (iron chloride)
Band-aids
Scissors and *tweezers* (both blunt and pointed)
Disinfectants for cleaning food and water dishes as well as the bath and the entire cage

Diseases

In a small book such as this I cannot discuss all the diseases your bird might conceivably get, and I will mention only the most common ones. A novice bird owner will have trouble

diagnosing the illness anyway, and I want to stress once more that if there is any doubt a veterinarian should be consulted.

Diseases of the Eyes
Symptoms: Inflamed conjunctivas, watery or pussy discharge, swollen tissue and crusty deposits around the eyes.
Cause: Drafts, smoke in the air, infections.
Treatment: Dab with a solution of boric acid or camomile extract, or apply antibiotic ointment (ophthalmic only!).

Fractures (Legs and Wings)
Symptoms: Hanging wing, inability to fly, favoring of injured limb.
Cause: Collision with window, etc.
Treatment: Wing fractures should be treated by a veterinarian. Fractures of the lower unfeathered leg can be treated by applying a splint made of a drinking straw and wrapping leg and

Figure 19 *Fractures of the wing bones call for a wing bandage.*

Diseases of Canaries

splint with adhesive tape (not too tightly). Place bird in infirmary cage for two to three weeks. Rest is important. Inexperienced bird owners should have the bird treated by a veterinarian.

Diarrhea and Enteritis
Symptoms: Watery, thin stool; dirty vent area; lack of appetite; lethargy.
Cause: Excitement (in this case the diarrhea will soon disappear), drafts, extreme changes in temperature, spoiled food.
Treatment: Warmth, 86–90°F (30–32°C). Infrared light, black tea, charcoal for birds. If infection is present, antibiotics and sulfonamides should be given, but only as prescribed by a veterinarian.

Obesity
Symptoms: Lethargy, unwillingness to fly, labored breathing, difficulties in molting.
Cause: Wrong diet, too much seed with high fat content (e.g., hemp and sunflower seeds), lack of exercise.
Treatment: Lower calorie diet (fruit, greens, millet seeds), lots of flying in an aviary or a period of free flying in the room at least once a day. Never make your bird fast!

Foot Problems
Symptoms: Scabs on legs and toes, protruding rough scales, favoring of one leg.
Cause: Unsanitary housing, dirty cage floor or perches, mites (see also *Scaly Legs*).
Treatment: Soften the scabs on feet and toes with warm water or camomile tea and remove carefully. Apply a very thin layer of topical ointment to the clean feet. Until the feet are completely healed remove sand or earth from bottom of cage. (Use newspapers or styrofoam instead.)

Viral Bird Plague
Symptoms: Severely labored breathing, diarrhea, fever, lack of appetite, paralysis, cramps, swelling of the eyelids; death within a few days.
Cause: Virus transmitted by wild birds or domestic fowl.
Treatment: Medication for canaries has not yet been developed. Prevent contact with sparrows and other wild birds, and roof in aviary as preventive measures.

Scaly Legs
Symptoms: Protruding foot and toe scales, whitish scabs along legs and toes, itching.
Cause: Mites that penetrate beneath the scales of feet and toes.
Treatment: Rub affected areas with scaly-leg ointment or Vaseline. In persistent cases, get a prescription ointment.

Diseases of Canaries

Canary Pox

Symptoms: Yellowish-white nodules or blisters on head, breast, wings, toes. Severely labored breathing, mucoid discharge, whitish deposit inside beak and on tongue.

Cause: Pox virus carried by newly bought birds or wild finches and sparrows.

Treatment: There is no treatment. If you have a fairly large number of birds, you should take the precautionary measure of having them vaccinated by a veterinarian. Thorough disinfection must follow any incidence of canary pox.

Coccidiosis

Symptoms: Slow wasting away, anorexia, diarrhea.

Cause: Coccidia (internal parasites). Large-scale infestations occur in warm and humid summer weather if bird cages are in unsanitary condition. Confirmation by laboratory stool analysis.

Treatment: Add sulfonamide or furazolidone to drinking water. Consult a veterinarian.

Egg Binding

Symptoms: Females sit around motionless and fluffed up. They often die within a few hours.

Cause: Mature egg is unable to pass through the vent, particularly in very young females. Sometimes the cause is that the egg shell did not form properly.

Treatment: Keep bird warm. Place a drop of salad oil near vent and massage vent and surrounding area gently. Be sure not to break the egg shell inside the bird. You can break the egg if it has not formed a shell, and you will be able to tell this by touch.

Mites

Symptoms: Restless sleep, continual preening and searching in the feathers, general decline.

Cause: Infestation with red bird mite, air sack mite, or feather mite, transmitted by newly acquired birds or wild birds. Red bird mites attack only at night; the other mites stay on the bird all the time.

Figure 20 *This is the correct way to hold your bird for examining him or cutting his nails. The head is placed between the index and middle finger; the wings are held by the thumb and little finger.*

Treatment: Use contact sprays available at pet stores. Apply spray to the aviary or cage, especially to hard-

49

to-get-at corners and cracks, as well as to the birds themselves. Don't spray eyes and beak. Hang anti-mite strips in the aviary or in the room where the birds are kept.

Rickets
Symptoms: Deformed feet, toes and wings, especially in young birds.
Cause: Vitamin D deficiency.
Treatment: Feed vitamin D_3. Different brands are available at pet stores.

Molting Problems (Soft Molt)
Symptoms: Birds molt unevenly, and the process is not completed in the normal molting period of four to six weeks. The birds look sickly and stop singing. New feathers are brittle and dull.
Cause: Incorrect or one-sided diet.
Treatment: Replace tap water with spring or uncarbonated mineral water and add minerals or a vitamin/mineral combination to drinking water and/or food.

Constipation
Symptoms: The bird sits on his perch apathetically and fluffed up. Attempts to pass stool are unsuccessful.
Cause: Food that was too old; ingestion of foreign bodies.
Treatment: Rub a little bit of warm

salad oil in and around the vent. Place a drop of castor oil or paraffin oil in the beak and make the bird swallow it. Feed fresh fruit and greens.

Overgrown Toe Nails
Symptoms: Toe nails are too long and curl in too much. Toes bend unnaturally. This is not really a disease, but the birds can no longer perch properly, and they easily get their claws caught.
Cause: Perches that are too smooth and too thin.
Treatment: Cut nails with sharp scissors or clippers about one eighth inch beyond the reddish blood vessels that are visible through the nail.

Birds are not easy patients to treat. This is particularly true of small birds like canaries. Birds have a high metabolic rate and therefore need to eat almost constantly. If they are weakened by illness they die very quickly. I have already mentioned that it is often too late for treatment by the time an illness has been noticed. The general rule that prevention is better than treatment is especially applicable to birds. If a bird is beyond help, it should be put to sleep by a veterinarian. If it is an imported bird and dies in your home, you should call a veterinarian or inform the state health authorities. If the cause of death is not clear, you should consult a veterinarian in any case. If you have other birds, you will want to know if the disease was an infectious one and take the appropriate precautions. Knowing the cause of death will also provide you with information useful in dealing with possible future emergencies.

Molting Season

Molting is not a disease but a normal process in a bird's life during which old, worn out feathers are replaced by new ones. But during molting, birds are particularly susceptible to disease. Also, poor diet or ill health can cause complications in the molting process. If this is the case, the bird will stop singing.

Molting consists of two phases: In one, the small contour feathers covering the body are replaced. In the other, the quills (the large wing and tail feathers), are shed and new ones grown.

Canaries normally molt in August and September. They replace all their feathers within six to eight weeks. If it takes much longer, something is wrong, i.e., there is some metabolic disorder which cannot be cured overnight. To molt properly, a bird must have had a good, varied diet rich in vitamins, minerals, and trace elements. If your bird does have difficulties molting, you can help somewhat by adding vitamin and mineral supplements available in pet stores to his water or food.

Canary Pairing and Breeding

If You Think You Want to Breed Canaries

Let me say first of all that a single canary that becomes attached to his human family is generally a lot more fun for the beginner than pairs of birds that are preoccupied primarily with each other and therefore pay little attention to people. Breeding canaries is for bird aficionados and demands specialized knowledge. It also requires more time and commitment because you are responsible not just for the original birds but also for the offspring. You will have to find homes for the young birds because you will neither want to nor be able to keep them all. And you can't give them to just anyone or, worse yet, release them into the wild. You have to find places for them where they are as well taken care of as they are with you.

Remember, too, that although breeding is part of the natural life cycle, each brood means wear and tear for the parent birds. If the breeder is intent on it, domestic birds like canaries can raise young more often during a mating season than birds in the wild. But the more often they are bred, the shorter their own life expectancy is.

You should breed canaries only if you can truthfully say that your birds are being properly kept. And this you can say only after you have had birds for a few years, and there have been no major illnesses or accidents.

In contrast to mating wild birds in captivity, which is rarely successful, breeding canaries is usually quite unproblematical. Still, there are some rules to be followed. I am not going to talk about all the possibilities for specialized breeds. Anyone with ambitions along those lines will have to accumulate knowledge in the course of years of experience or consult more specialized treatises (see Books for Further Information, page 73). This little book is meant only for beginners who may want to raise a batch of young birds or find themselves doing so by accident. I will therefore describe only the easiest and most common methods of breeding.

The "Normal" Method

Wild canaries pair and live together monogamously during the mating season. It would therefore seem only natural to keep caged canaries in pairs. You can in fact keep a pair in an indoor or outdoor aviary or—if the two birds take to each other—in a cage approximately 3½ × 2 × 1½ feet (100 × 40 × 60 cm). But you cannot take for granted that they will take to each other. A canary will not accept just any other canary as a mate. Birds feel sympathy and antipathy just as we do. If a male and a female do not like each other, you will soon know it. They will keep chasing each other away from the food and from perches. If you have such an incompatible pair, you should separate them quickly because otherwise the weaker of the two will start wasting away.

If you do have a compatible pair, there is considerable advantage in keeping the two birds together. As in the wild, the male will feed his mate before and during brooding, and later he will help feed the nestlings. He will often take over the feeding of the young completely when they start to fly. By then the female is usually busy building a new nest. Canaries generally build a new nest for each clutch

Figure 21 *Canaries that start fighting should be separated quickly.*

of eggs, though they will occasionally reuse an old one. Because of the danger of parasites you should remove the old nests as soon as the young birds leave them.

If a well-matched pair is allowed to live together, the female is likely to be a good brooder, and the young grow up under optimal conditions. This is not necessarily the case if you remove the male after mating.

One Male and Several Females

You can also keep one male together with three or four females in one large aviary. But in this situation it can happen that two females bother each other while building their nests or while brooding if they have chosen nesting sites that are too close to each other. Also, if you want to breed a special strain (see page 7), you have to be careful that all your birds are of the same pure breed. Otherwise this harem-like setup can produce the most unpredictable results.

Multiple Brooding Boxes

This method is used primarily by experienced breeders. The females are kept separately in small brooder cages. The breeder places a male with a female when she is ready to breed and has built her nest. As soon as she has finished laying her clutch of eggs, the male is removed and put with another female. This method presupposes that the breeder can tell exactly when the female is ready to mate, and the beginner will rarely have that kind of know-how. Another drawback is that the female will sometimes abandon her eggs. If she does hatch them, she will then have to raise the young by herself, which represents a severe strain for her. Females kept in brooding boxes should therefore not raise more than two broods a year. Single pairs or several females kept together with a male who will be able to assist with the feeding can usually raise three broods a year without damage to their health.

Disturbances to Brooding

The best way to prevent difficulties during the brooding and raising of young birds is to keep the parents separate from other birds. Even in a relatively harmonious coexistence with other small granivorous birds in an aviary unpleasant incidents can occur. There can be fights over nesting sites, or nesting material is stolen from right under the sitting female. The nest will get shallower and shallower until the eggs roll out of the nest or are crushed by the female sitting on them. Outdoor aviaries harbor even more dangers. Other birds can be a

Figure 22 *Here is a homemade indoor aviary that fits in harmoniously with the living room decor and provides enough space for several pairs of canaries to breed.*

◁ Plate 8   *Two African relatives of the canary from the Canary Islands.*
Above: Yellow-Bellied Canary (Serinobs flaviventris). *This bird is found from Rhodesia to Cape Town.*
Below: Sulfur-Yellow Canary (Crithagra sulphurata), *found from Central to South Africa.*

nuisance. Mice and rats may steal not only nesting materials but even eggs or newly hatched birds. Cats or other predators might reach down to the nest if it is built too close to the top of the aviary and make a meal of the sitting female. Or the driving rain during a storm might drench the nest and its occupants, causing the female to abandon it.

Bringing a Pair Together

Figure 23   *The climax of canary courtship is the act of mating, which lasts for only a fraction of a second.*

Generally you will start out with a male because males sing. After several months or even years, when your male is completely established and feels at home in his cage or aviary, you may decide you would like to raise some young canaries. You go out, buy a female canary, bring her home, put her in with the male, and expect nature to take her course. You will probably be in for a big surprise. The female is petrified and intimidated by her new surroundings. Love is the farthest thing from her mind. The male, on the other hand, is totally at home in his cage, is forward, and starts chasing the female. This is hardly a propitious beginning for a bird marriage. Two birds that don't know each other must have time to get acquainted before they will pair.

The breeding season for canaries begins in the spring. Breeders usually exhibit their birds in the fall when molting is over and the plumage is at its best and brightest. This is when they sell the birds they are not going to use for breeding purposes, and this is the best time to buy a female for breeding. In the course of the winter, she will have time to get used to her new home and make friends with her prospective mate.

When you bring your new bird home, do not put it with its intended partner right away. House the birds separately but so that they can see and hear each other. Gradually bring them closer together. When all signs of shyness and aggression have disappeared it is time to move them together. As spring progresses the male will begin his courtship by feeding the female and singing constantly. When the female is ready to mate, she will crouch on a perch and let the male "ride" her (Figure 23). Soon thereafter she will start building her nest.

Nesting Materials

A clean cage or aviary offers no nesting materials. No bird can build a nest out of sand. And even if nesting materials could be found, there is no place to build the nest. So you must be sure that nesting receptacles (Figure 24) are provided as soon as the birds need them. You can buy various types of receptacles, some designed for suspending, others for resting on a surface. Not all are equally practical. Receptacles that are hemispheric in shape and made of bamboo, wire, or plastic netting are usually accepted by canaries and work out well. If the receptacles are solid, i.e., without slits or holes, the nesting material cannot

be properly secured, no matter what the receptacle is made of. If the female catches her toe in a nest that is not "tied down," she may, in her attempt to get free, knock the nest down, eggs and all.

Woven baskets are open at the top, and since canaries build open nests, you can watch the whole breeding cycle from the laying and hatching of the eggs to the maturing of the young birds.

If you have an outdoor aviary, you have to place the nesting receptacles where wind and rain will not get at them. Nest baskets come in various sizes from 3½ to 5½ inches (8 to 13 cm) in diameter to accommodate different canary breeds. Canaries also like cave-like holes in wood for nesting, as in a hollow tree. Plastic is not good for this purpose because the nest cannot adhere to it the way it can to a rough wooden surface. Of course, the nest is not as likely to fall out of a cave-like structure as it is out of a basket.

Receptacles should be located in the upper-half of the aviary. If you use a cage, the receptacle with its brood cage (Figure 24) is attached outside a door opening but right up against it. This way the opening is blocked; the nest will not take up room inside the cage; and you will be able to check it without having to reach inside the cage.

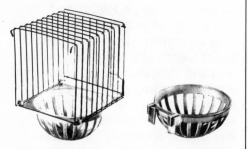

Figure 24 *Plastic nest receptacle with and without a nest box.*

Canary Pairing and Breeding

The *nesting material* should be as varied as possible. Provide sturdier materials first to insure the stability of the nest. The materials must be of proper size. Canaries cannot build a nest out of large twigs and branches. More useful are short cotton threads (birds can get caught or even strangle in long ones), coconut fiber, sisal, and hay. In an outdoor aviary, birds will also find and incorporate tiny feathers, fine grass, all kinds of plant fibers, and other soft things to line the inside of the nest. A good selection of appropriate nesting materials makes it more likely that the female will sit on the eggs and hatch them. A variety of building materials also makes the nest tighter and more solid, which is important for the safety of the eggs and the nestlings.

The Laying of the Eggs

As soon as the nest is finished, the female will lay her first egg. This usually happens in the early morning. Wild finches do not start sitting on the eggs until the clutch is complete. Wild canaries are the same way. But in the course of domestication this behavior has changed, and the tame canary usually starts brooding almost as soon as she has laid her first egg. Since the four to six eggs are laid a day apart, they will, after an incubation of thir-

teen to fourteen days, hatch over a period of several days. The oldest nestling may be six days old by the time the last is hatched. The late-comers have little chance in the competition for food, and it is therefore advisable to see to it that the whole brood hatches on the same day. This is not difficult to do. Simply take each

Figure 25 *If the canary couple remains together during the brooding period, the male will feed the female with food from his crop.*

egg out of the nest as soon as it is laid and replace it with a fake egg of plastic or plaster of Paris. Keep the real eggs in a small box lined with something soft and place it in a safe but airy spot. When the bird has laid her third or fourth egg, put all the eggs back in the nest. Now chances are that the whole brood will hatch at more or less the same time. Of course you have to handle the eggs that you temporarily remove carefully. Don't shake them or knock them about, and protect them from heat and cold. And don't chase the female off her nest when you take away an egg. Approach the nest quietly. At some point she will probably leave the nest, or, if she is very tame, you can nudge her gently. If that does not work, carefully reach into the nest with two fingers. But be very cautious; the eggs are very fragile and can easily be crushed.

In the finch family — and that includes the canaries — only the female sits on the eggs. She leaves them briefly in the morning and evening to relieve herself and to drink water. If there is no male present, she also eats at that time. If the couple live together, the male will bring food to the nest and feed her from his crop.

Ordinarily canaries are good brooders, though there are exceptions. These may occur in the case of inexperienced females or if the brooding instinct is not fully developed. Occasionally a female may be so nervous that she leaves the nest at the slightest disturbance. Keep such a bird as quiet as possible, and leave her alone as much as you can. If she is sitting in a small cage, move it to an out-of-the-way spot. Some females, particularly young ones who are sitting for the first time, will leave the nest in the middle of brooding. They have had enough. Breeders who have a number of broody birds can put the

eggs under another hen whose eggs are due to hatch about the same time. If you cannot provide such a substitute mother, all you can do is hope for better luck next time. If a bird turns out to be a generally unreliable brooder, you will have to exchange her.

Some or all of the eggs may not be fertilized. You can tell after the fourth day of incubation by holding them up against a light. Use a flashlight or light bulb. In a fertilized egg you will see the embryo as a dark spot with tiny red blood vessels. Unfertilized eggs are uniformly transparent. Even if all the eggs are unfertile you should let the female sit the whole period of about two weeks so that the normal rhythm of the breeding cycle is not upset.

Unfertilized eggs are not uncommon. Wild birds living in their natural habitat also lay unfertile eggs. But if you find that a couple consistently has unfertile eggs, you will have to try substituting first another male, then another female. If you have no luck either way, you will have to get a new pair of birds.

Hatching of the Young

The young will hatch after thirteen or fourteen days. Now the female has to keep the nestlings warm and feed

Canary Pairing and Breeding

them. Canaries usually make good mothers, feeding the nestlings soft, predigested food from their crops. If the father is present, he will provide the female with food which she will pass on to the young. At this phase, too, the father plays an important role, which is an added reason for keeping pairs together.

If a female is a poor mother, you will have to give up on the young. Hand-rearing is not advisable, especially for the beginner. It would be too difficult and probably unsuccessful, because the baby birds are so tiny and need predigested food.

One factor contributing to the successful raising of young birds is the rearing food (see page 42). This is a high protein food that is available in pet or bird stores in a ready-to-feed mixture. It should be added to the regular diet of the adult birds at the beginning of the brooding period. Once the young have hatched, it is more important than ever that all the food be fresh and uncontaminated. When the nestlings are a few days old the female will start leaving the nest, and the male will now also feed the young directly.

Around the sixth day, pin feathers begin to appear and give the baby birds an almost hedgehog-like look. Six days later, the feathers have fully developed and cover the birds with a warm coat. By the seventeenth or eighteenth day the birds are ready to leave the nest. The parents will still

Figure 26 *Even after the young have left the nest, the parents often continue to feed them for quite some time.*

feed them — though the young will also eat on their own — until the young become completely independent. As I have already said, the female will often start building a new nest while the male is still feeding the fledglings. As soon as the young birds are no longer dependent on the parents, they can be removed and housed in cages of their own.

Understanding Canaries

The following chapter is intended to help you understand your canary better. This will be of benefit to you as well as to your pet. Like any other creature, your canary has patterns of behavior typical of his species, and understanding them will help you tell how he is feeling at any given time. Is he healthy or sick? Tired and wanting to be left alone or active and ready to communicate with his human partner? Try to look at your feathered friend from a bird's point of view for a while, and you will find it much easier to understand his particular situation. To start with, I want to explain the physical make-up of birds.

What Exactly Is a Bird?

Birds are vertebrates that are physically distinguishable from other members of this class by the presence of feathers. There is no such thing as a naked bird, unless you count a

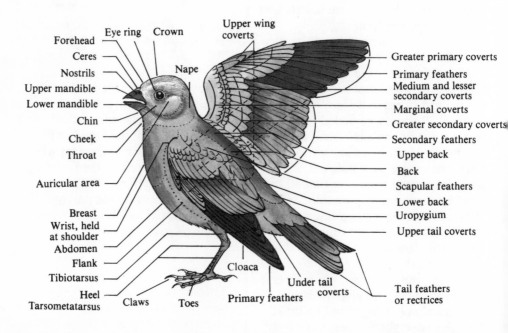

Figure 27 *What's what on a canary? Knowledge of bird anatomy and feather terminology can be useful if you have to confer with your veterinarian.*

plucked chicken. Instead of arms or forelegs, a bird has wings. A few birds have, in the course of their evolution, lost the ability to fly: the ostrich, for example. Others, like the penguin, no longer use their wings for flying but only for propelling themselves in the water. But the large majority of birds fly, and their bodies have acquired several "aerodynamic" features. Thus, the feathers not only maintain body temperature; they also even out irregular body structure and contribute to the streamlined shape necessary for flying. The bones of birds are strong but light, and some of them are hollow. Even the big beaks of some species contain more air than anyone might guess by looking at them. And there are air sacks that reach from the lungs and separate the large flying muscles from other parts of the body. These sacks are a kind of cooling system and keep the muscles from overheating during flight.

Birds' feathers are made up of a horny substance similar to that of scales in reptiles. Birds are descended from reptiles. The prototypical bird *Archaeopteryx* that dates back about 150 million years to the Jurassic period and whose fossilized remains were discovered in Bavaria represents a stage somewhere between reptile and bird. It still had a long tail made up of vertebrae, jaws with teeth, and claws on its fingers, but it also had the feathers and wings of a bird. Modern birds have horny scales only on their legs, and their bony beaks are covered with a horny layer.

Birds, like mammals, are warm-blooded. Their normal body temperature is about 106°F (41°C). Variations in external temperature are largely compensated for by the plumage. If the bird is too warm, it folds its feathers close to the body. When there is no air between the feathers, there is no insulating effect. If the bird gets cold, it fluffs up its feathers. The air between them is heated by body warmth, and the bird is covered with a nice layer of insulation.

Birds have no sweat glands and therefore cannot perspire. If they want to cool down, they let moisture evaporate from the throat. They open their beaks and pant just as dogs, which also lack sweat glands, do.

All birds lay eggs with solid shells made up of calcium. They sit on their eggs and raise their brood themselves. Only a few brood parasites, of which the cuckoo is the best known, leave the hatching and raising of the young to foster parents. Incubator birds *(Megapodiidae)* bury their eggs in warm sand or in a pile of leaves. Sunshine and the heat generated by the fermentation process take the place

Understanding Canaries

of the parent's body warmth. When the young hatch, they make their way toward the daylight and immediately start fending for themselves. But these are, as I have said, exceptions.

You will be particularly interested in the feeding habits and digestion of birds. The popular assumption that birds have to eat practically all the time is quite correct. Birds have to eat about a third of their body weight every day, and a small bird can die within a few hours is it is deprived of food, particularly in cold weather.

The food is digested very quickly, and undigested material is excreted through the vent or cloaca, an opening that also serves for eliminating urine and for reproductive functions. Bird droppings almost always leave stains on upholstery and clothes. Consequently you should put a tissue or rag on your shoulder — if that is your bird's favorite spot — or wherever else it likes to perch.

Birds are visual creatures, orienting themselves primarily by sight. Their sense of hearing is also very acute, but their sense of smell is not very well developed. Only vultures have keen noses. They can tell from afar if there is any carrion around. The sense of taste is well developed in birds. They will eat only what they like. But since they spot their food first with their eyes, a blind bird is doomed.

How Wild Canaries Live

In the zoological classification system the wild canary is assigned to the serins, which form part of the finch family *(Fringillidae),* which belongs to the genus *Passeres,* which is, in turn, a suborder of the *Passeriformes* or perching birds. Our domestic canary has all the qualities of his relatives, and as long as he was just a greenish bird hopping around in the trees and bushes of his native Canary Islands there was nothing remarkable about him. He became famous only when man had succeeded, by selective breeding, in turning him into the spectacularly colored pet bird we know today.

The wild canary *(Serinus canaria canaria)* occurs naturally on the Canary Islands, on Madeira, and in the Azores. It is somewhat smaller than most of the domestic breeds, measuring about 5½ inches (13 cm) from the beak to the tip of the tail. The yellow color typical of domestic canaries also occurs in their wild cousins, but here it is mixed in with yellowish green, plain green, and darker colors. The females are brownish gray and more subdued in color than the males. The wild canary is also closely related to the European serin *(Serinus serinus).* The two species can be crossbred quite easily and produce fertile offspring.

Understanding Canaries

Opinions concerning the quality of the wild canary's song differ. Some claim they like the song of the wild bird better than that of the domesticated canary. Others maintain the opposite view. Basically all the elements that go into the song of the Roller (see page 8) are present in the wild bird's song. But it also contains less "beautiful" notes, if you judge by human standards. Of course, a bird could care less whether his song appeals to human ears; it is, after all, meant for other birds.

Each bird has the voice that is characteristic of its species, and all it wants to achieve with it is to assert its territory, attract a mate, and drive away rivals.

For a bird living in the wild the mating season consists of a series of behavior patterns and the presence of certain environmental conditions. If any one factor is absent, there will be no offspring. Certain physiological conditions must exist for the sexual instinct to assert itself in the spring. The birds must be physically mature and in good health.

Mating season for wild canaries in their native habitat begins in February or March, when the singing of the male becomes more intense. The males also perform courtship displays similar to the ones we can observe in our small finches. Without interrupt-ing their song they flutter back and forth between trees. As soon as the male and the female have accepted each other, the female begins to build a nest. She chooses a forked branch near a tree trunk about six to nine feet (2–3 m) from the ground. Using plant fibers, grass, and other soft materials, she constructs a nest shaped like a deep bowl. Then she lays three to five eggs and sits on them for thirteen days. The male provides her with food. Both parents take part in the rearing of the young. Often a second, and sometimes a third, brood follows the first within one breeding season. When the last fledglings are independent and mature, the canaries gather in large flocks and roam over the island all winter in search of food.

The mortality rate of young canaries is high. The time between hatching and becoming self-sufficient is fraught with danger, and only a small number of the young live to sexual maturity. This is not unusual for small birds. The continued existence of a species is assured if two offspring survive their parents. Enemies are everywhere: Birds of prey, predatory mammals, and snakes all hunt young birds. But many fledglings also perish during their first flying efforts or in periods of bad weather.

Understanding Canaries

Behavioral Patterns of the Domestic Canary

The life of the domestic canary differs considerably from that of its cousin in the wild. The pet canary always has plenty to eat (unless you forget to feed him); he doesn't have to worry about enemies (unless you have an untrustworthy cat); and, if he is not kept in a communal aviary, there is no need to defend territory. In short, he has little opportunity to practice his innate skills. He eats, drinks, hops and flies around, sleeps, and preens himself. There is not much else to do for a bird in a cage. Who can tell if a canary misses the life of his ancestors? Luckily he lacks the ability to reflect on his fate. But probably he is perfectly content. Canaries are not very sociable. There are definitely sociable and unsociable birds, depending on their breed. Sociability in this case is not a matter of character, as it is for people, but of biology and the behavioral characteristics of the species. Birds that in the wild live in large social groups, or flocks, will form attachments to others of their kind or to surrogates even in captivity. They may choose their human caretaker, for instance. Many kinds of birds belong to this sociable type, most notably, perhaps, the families that include the starlings, the jackdaws, and the parakeets (especially the lovebird). These birds need company to be happy. If they are kept in isolation without something to do and without stimulation, they will pine away.

Wild canaries, and consequently domestic ones, are fairly unsociable birds. Actually they are rather hard to classify. During the mating season the pairs live in clearly defined territories that are defended against other members of the species. In the fall, after the mating season, canaries, both young and old, form great flocks. These flocks, however, stay together only for the winter and are more of a protective alliance against common enemies than true communities with "personal" bonds between different members. Unlike jackdaws, individual canaries in a flock probably do not even recognize each other.

In the mating season not every wild canary is able to find a mate, and some have to go without offspring. This is probably a factor that contributes to the suitability of the canary for a pet, because you can leave him alone occasionally without having to worry about his well-being. That does not mean, of course, that a canary does not care one way or the other. Every animal, no matter how

Understanding Canaries

unsociable, gets used to the routine of its living conditions and learns from it. A canary learns very quickly who gives him food, water, and treats and keeps him company. This may sound like a contradiction of what I said earlier, but this is not the case. Animals need a certain amount of activity around them, some excitement, so to speak, to make life worth living. This keeps them alert and lively; it stimulates their circulatory and metabolic systems. That is why your canary likes it if you are around, as long as you don't scare him or drive him crazy by having the TV on full blast or turn everything topsy turvy. But, to be candid, you will never develop the kind of relationship with a canary that you would with a lovebird.

Figure 28 *To make a canary tame enough to come to your hand, you have to feed him regularly and be generous with your other attentions to him.*

There is one possible exception, and that is if the canary has been hand-raised by the owner. This is unlikely in the case of a beginner. A hand-raised canary that never knew its parents will conceive of the human being as one of its own kind. After all, it does not know that a human being is a human being. It only "knows" innately and instinctively that the creature that feeds it and keeps it warm as a nestling must be of its own kind. That is the way it is in nature.

Sounds and Body Language

If a canary thinks of a person as another canary, it will treat him or her accordingly. It will perform courtship displays for its caretaker if it is a male, or it will indicate its readiness to mate if it is a female. In all this, the canary does not "see" the whole, large human being. Usually it is interested only in the head and face. Apparently, for creatures like birds that orient themselves primarily by sight, the eyes are the identifying feature of the head. Birds in the wild, particularly a pair, will sit next to each other on a branch. A human-impressed, or even just a tame, canary will also try to sit so that his head is side to side with that of the human. That is why he likes to perch on your shoulder. There he is close to your head and your eyes, and he can get a good foothold. The shoulder is also a favorite landing spot. It offers a good view, the bird is high up, and the head of the partner is close by, but the hand is at a safe distance. Because the bird has probably had the unpleasant experience at one time or another of the human hand catching or grabbing him, it is understandable that he does not quite trust the hand.

Figure 29 *The owner's shoulder is the best place for making eye contact.*

But in one case the bird's distrust for the human hand is absent, i.e., when a hand-raised bird courts the person it conceives of as a mate. I have already said that humans are too large to be taken in as a whole by the little canary. Its natural mate would be its own size. In looking for something closer to its own size in the human partner, the bird hits on the hand. Some of the reasons for this choice may be that the hand seems

more like an independent entity because it is very mobile and clearly distinguishable from the rest of the person. Also, the hand feeds and pets, can be jumped on and snuggled into. In all these respects it resembles a true partner more than any other part of the human anatomy.

So you will know what it means when a canary cock struts up and down in front of your hand, sings at it, jumps on it, and presses its rear against it, or if a hen nestles up close to it in a crouched position. Be glad that your bird likes you so much. But I have to repeat that this degree of closeness between canary and human is extremely rare. If the relationship between bird and human is not as close — and that is generally the rule — the canary will look for another substitute to court and attempt to mate with. This could be its image in a mirror, a little yellow ball, or some other small object. None of this does any harm. On the contrary, it keeps the bird occupied in a more or less natural manner.

Your bird will become tame and trusting only if you approach it quietly and patiently. The degree of your success depends on many factors. Since canaries have been domesticated for centuries, they are not as shy as caged wild birds. The constant vigilance against potential

Understanding Canaries

enemies has practically been bred out of them. Still, the amount of trust toward humans is affected by how young a bird is when you acquire him and whether he was raised in an outdoor aviary or an indoor one where he had a lot of human contact from the beginning. It also depends on whether you pay a lot of attention to him or simply feed him once a day. If you don't know the background of a pet you cannot know if his previous experience with humans was good or bad and to what extent it has marked his character. But whatever his history, your canary will soon recognize you as his source of food. Once you know what treats he likes, you have found a good means to tame him and even to get him to eat from your

Figure 30 *Canaries "make themselves scarce" when they are frightened. The body stretches out, and the feathers cling closely to it.*

hand. But I want to stress again: Don't try to catch or grab him unless absolutely necessary (to cut his claws, for instance, page 50). A bird does not like to be handled. If you want something to pet and scratch and thump, get yourself a dog or a cat or a guinea pig, not a bird.

One reason for this is that a bird's plumage is very delicate and not meant to be tampered with. It serves functions that are crucial to the bird's survival. That is why the bird keeps it in top condition by constant grooming and preening. He will get upset if the feathers are even slightly disarrayed. Preening may appear like a haphazard pecking and scratching, but it is in fact an important activity that always produces a smooth coat of feathers. If you interfere, thinking he will like scratching the way a cat or dog does, he will be far from enthused. What you have accomplished is chaos of the worst kind, as you would quickly recognize if you were to look at the feathers under a microscope. Your canary will have to spend hours restoring order and repairing the damage of broken and split feathers.

There is another reason why birds don't like to be touched. In nature, being grabbed means certain death. If a bird of prey gets hold of a small bird the way you do, that spells the

69

Understanding Canaries

end. Your canary will therefore instinctively avoid any situation where he is deprived of his freedom of movement. If you insist on physical contact with your bird, experiment to see if he likes to be stroked gently on his head or throat with a fingernail or a match stick. Occasionally a bird will not object to this. If he doesn't like it, he will move or fly off. Many birds engage in communal preening. That is, they stroke each other with their beaks, preferably on parts of the body that are hard for them to reach themselves. Even the most agile bird cannot scratch his head with his beak. This mutual preening presupposes great trust, since the proximity necessary for it would mean vulnerability to an attack.

Don't ever try to touch your bird against his will, let alone catch him. That would be the surest way to teach him to avoid your hands. But you don't need to touch your bird to enjoy him. Just sit down near him and watch him for a while. Observe what he does, and observe carefully. In this way you will soon get to know and understand your canary better.

Is Your Bird Relaxed or Scared?

You can tell by his feathers whether your canary is relaxed or scared, whether in good health or sickly. A sick bird will sit still and all fluffed up. The eyes are usually closed and the breathing heavy. A scared bird looks sleek and smooth. His feathers are folded close to his body; he is ready to take off at the slightest provocation. A bird never flies with ruffled feathers; there would be too much air resistance. In its normal state, i.e., when the bird is relaxed, the feathers are neither fluffed up nor completely smoothed down. The bird is in casual attire, you might say.

How the Bird Sleeps

Not all birds bury their heads in their back feathers to sleep. Some simply hunch the head down between the shoulders with the beak pointing

Figure 31 *Typical sleeping posture of canaries. Remember that a bird, too, needs undisturbed sleep to stay healthy.*

forward. But songbirds, like many other birds, sleep with their heads buried in the back feathers. Usually the feathers are fluffed up to hold the heat, and often one leg is pulled up. A mechanism involving the muscles and tendons of the leg keeps birds from falling while they are asleep. When the knee and ankle bend, the toes automatically bend, too, and grab the perch tightly. A canary never sleeps during the day, unless it feels very secure. In nature no small bird can afford to close its eyes during daylight. There are too many enemies around. But at night a canary sleeps so soundly that you could pick it up with your hand. Don't do it, however, because it might get even more frightened than during the day.

Preening

I have already said that preening is of the utmost importance. When preening itself, the bird follows a definite pattern that is inborn, but it probably also learns some refinements in the course of a lifetime. The beak and the claws on the toes are used for preening, and the feathers are smoothed out in the process. Preening takes up the best part of the day. In order to reach the throat feathers with the beak, the bird has to stretch the neck and at the same time bend the head in such a way that the chin folds back against the throat. This is quite a strenuous exercise, and it is usually performed with eyes closed. The tip of the beak takes each little feather in turn and places it just right. The same is done with all the contour feathers. The toes are used in places where the beak will not reach, such as the cheeks, the back of the neck, and the top of the head. The bird will, for instance, pick up his left leg and slightly extend the left wing, then move the leg between the body and the wing and start scratching. Behavioral scientists call this scratching "from behind." All songbirds do this. Other kinds of birds scratch "from the front," i.e., instead of spreading the wing, they reach the claws around it. The large wing and tail feathers are pulled through the beak one by one. During molting time, loose feathers can come out in the process of preening.

Figure 32 *The care of his plumage is one of a canary's most important occupations. He uses his beak and his nails for preening.*

Understanding Canaries

Preening usually culminates in a vigorous shake, which fluffs up the feathers. This, too, aids the proper arrangement of the plumage. When the feathers are fluffed up, they are evenly spaced, and they will lie down in place when the bird makes itself sleek.

Figure 33 *If a canary stretches his wings and legs while preening that is a sign of well-being. Frequently a yawn will accompany this activity.*

The canary will preen itself with special care after a bath. It likes to bathe daily to keep its body and feathers clean. A bath can get rather turbulent. The bird's wings beat wildly in the water, and water sprays over the entire small body of the bird. Afterwards, the feathers are wet and not exactly tidy. The bird now has to smooth and rearrange his feathers as well as dry them. That takes time. The feathers are kept supple and water-repellent with a fatty secretion from the preen gland located just in front of the tail. The bird uses his beak to remove the secretion from the gland and distributes it all over the feathers.

Preening is usually combined with stretching movements. The wings and legs are stretched back away from the body. A bird uses stretching just as we do when we feel stiff. And he even knows how to yawn. Considering these similarities between canaries and people, we should not find it too difficult to understand canaries.

Books for Further Information

Canaries in Color
George Lynch: Sterling

How Birds Work: A Guide to Bird Biology
Ron Freethy: Sterling

Songbirds
Time-Life Book Editors: Time-Life

Index

Index

Perfect for Pet Owners!

"Clear, concise... written in simple, nontechnical language."

—Booklist

BARRON'S

CATS! CATS! CATS! CATS! CATS!
CATS! CATS! CATS! CATS! CATS!

BARRON'S CAT FANCIER'S SERIES

These gloriously illustrated books by professional breeders celebrate three of the world's most exalted cats: the Longhair, the Burmese and the Siamese. Each one is filled with information of special interest to owners and breeders, including a history of the breed and its development, shows, breeding, cat clubs, and much, much more. The authoritative texts are enriched by dozens of attractive, appealing photographs, most in color. Each book paperback,
64 pp., 8" x 8¼"

LONGHAIR CATS
Grace Pond
(2923-2)

SIAMESE CATS
Mary Dunnill
(2924-0)

BURMESE CATS
Moira K. Swift
(2925-9)

BARRON'S
250 Wireless Boulevard, Hauppauge, NY 11788